MATTER AND MATERIALS

Clare Hibbert

Enslow Publishing
101 W. 23rd Street
Suite 240
New York, NY 10011
USA

enslow.com

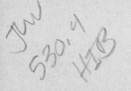

Published in 2019 by Enslow Publishing, LLC.
101 W. 23rd Street, Suite 240, New York, NY 10011

Cataloging-in-Publication Data

Names: Hibbert, Clare.
Title: Matter and materials / Clare Hibbert.
Description: New York : Enslow Publishing, 2019. | Series: Science explorers | Includes glossary and index.
Identifiers: ISBN 9781978506725 (pbk.) | ISBN 9781978506459 (library bound) | ISBN 9781978506800 (6pack)
| ISBN 9781978506527 (ebook)
Subjects: LCSH: Matter—Juvenile literature. | Matter—Properties—Juvenile literature. | Materials—Juvenile literature.
Classification: LCC QC173.36 H625 2019 | DDC 530.4—dc23

Printed in the United States of America

To Our Readers: We have done our best to make sure all website addresses in this book were active and appropriate when we went to press. However, the author and the publisher have no control over and assume no liability for the material available on those websites or on any websites they may link to. Any comments or suggestions can be sent by email to customerservice@enslow.com.

Photo Credits:
Every attempt has been made to clear copyright. Should there be any inadvertent omission, please apply to the publisher for rectification.
Key: b-bottom, t-top, c-center, l-left, r-right
NASA Images: 15br; Science Photo Library: 4–5 (Photo Insolite Realite), 9cl (Tony McConnell), 10cl & 32 br (Dr Gary Settles), 12l (GIPhotoStock), 18–19 (Matthew Oldfield), 22–23 (Patrice Loiez, CERN); Shutterstock: cover main & 8–9 (Sebastian Janicki), cover cl (topseller), cover tr & 16tr & 30br (Sebastian Janicki), cover bl & 18cl (Taras Vyshnya), cover tr & 22bl (Andrea Danti), cover br & 17tl (yongyut rukkachatsuwa), 4tr (adriaticfoto), 4c (Neal Pritchard Media), 4br (YC_Chee), 5tr (adike), 5br (NASA Images), 6–7 (ZinaidaSopina), 6tr (MicroOne), 6bl & 31br (sandatlas.org), 7bl (kaer_stock), 8cl (grafvision), 9bl (Macrovector), 10–11 (Digital Storm), 10bl (MilanMarkovic78), 11tl (Evgeniya Chertova), 12–13 (Fredy Thuerig), 13cr (Inna Bigun), 13bl (NoPainNoGain), 14–15 (Maximilian Laschon), 15tl (NoPainNoGain), 16–17 (Mark Agnor), 17bl (Andrey_Kuzmin), 18bl (Designua), 19bl (CE Wagstaff/Georgios Kolidas), 20–21 (cyo bo), 20tr (haryigit), 21cr (patx64), 23cr (MichaelTaylor), 23bl (mila kad), 24–25 (Protasov AN), 24bl (Inna Bigun), 25br (Larina Marina), 26tr (agrofruti), 26tl (agarose), 26cr (Faezah), 26bl (beibaoke), 26br (Malachy666), 27tl (Tanguy de Saint-Cyr), 27tr (Sherbak_photo), 27cl (Rawpixel.com), 27br (railway fx), 27bl (Oleg Peresvet), 28br (Ruth Swan), 29cr (Bjoern Wylezich), 29bl (Roy Harris); Wikimedia Commons: 21tl (Christian Albrecht Jensen), 25tl (Nobel Foundation).

CONTENTS

Introduction 4

Phases of Matter 6

Solid Materials 8

Liquids and Gases 10

Elements 12

Periodic Table 14

Rocks and Minerals 16

Chemistry at Work 18

Electrical Properties 20

Inside the Atom 22

Quantum World..................................... 24

Fun Facts 26

Your Questions Answered 28

Glossary 30

Further Information 31

Index 32

Introduction

Science is amazing! It shapes our understanding of the universe and has transformed our everyday lives. At its heart, science is a way of collecting facts, developing ideas to explain those facts, and making predictions we can test.

Laboratory Learning

Chemistry investigates materials, from solids, liquids, and gases to the tiny atoms that make up everything. By understanding the rules behind how different kinds of matter behave, we can create new chemicals and materials with amazing properties.

Scientists can observe chemical reactions under a microscope.

Secrets of the Universe

Physics is the scientific study of energy, forces, mechanics, and waves. Energy includes heat, light, and electricity. Physics also looks at the structure of atoms and the workings of the universe. Even the galaxies obey the laws of physics!

Chimpanzees are one of around 7.8 million species of living animals.

Many forms of energy are involved in a storm.

Life on Earth

Natural history is the study of living things—the countless plants, animals, and other creatures that inhabit Earth now or which existed in the past. It studies how these organisms are influenced by each other and their environment. It also looks at the complex process of evolution—gradual change from one generation to the next.

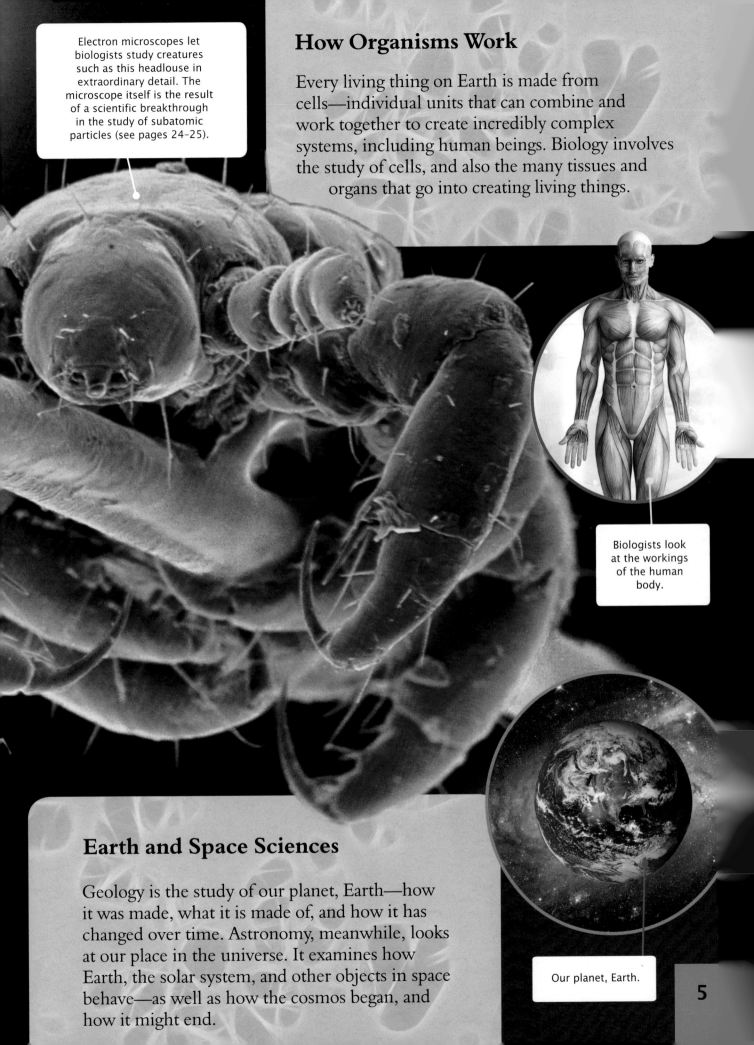

Electron microscopes let biologists study creatures such as this headlouse in extraordinary detail. The microscope itself is the result of a scientific breakthrough in the study of subatomic particles (see pages 24–25).

How Organisms Work

Every living thing on Earth is made from cells—individual units that can combine and work together to create incredibly complex systems, including human beings. Biology involves the study of cells, and also the many tissues and organs that go into creating living things.

Biologists look at the workings of the human body.

Earth and Space Sciences

Geology is the study of our planet, Earth—how it was made, what it is made of, and how it has changed over time. Astronomy, meanwhile, looks at our place in the universe. It examines how Earth, the solar system, and other objects in space behave—as well as how the cosmos began, and how it might end.

Our planet, Earth.

Phases of Matter

Matter is the stuff that makes up the universe. It is built from countless tiny particles called atoms and molecules. Depending on how these particles arrange themselves and join together, matter can take one of three forms: solid, liquid, or gas. These forms are called phases.

Material Bonds

Solid substances are made up of particles joined by strong, rigid bonds. Particles in liquids have looser bonds, which constantly break and reform. Gases are very loose collections of atoms or molecules that have extremely weak bonds. The strength of a material's bonds affects its ability to keep its shape.

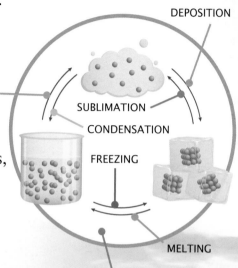

DEPOSITION

EVAPORATION

SUBLIMATION

CONDENSATION

FREEZING

MELTING

Water can be a solid (ice), liquid, or gas (steam). When it's solid, it stays the same shape whatever container it's put in. As a liquid, its molecules flow outward to spread across surfaces. Steam spreads to fill its container or heads in all directions.

Changing Phases

The phase of a substance is affected by how much energy its individual particles have to move around, and this energy depends on the material's temperature. Heating a solid material enough loosens its bonds and makes it melt. Heating a liquid will cause particles to boil or evaporate into a gas.

Different substances have different melting and boiling points. The melting point of rock is very high, so molten lava rapidly turns solid when it erupts from a volcano and begins to cool.

A geyser is created where matter suddenly changes its phase.

As the steam meets the cold air above, it cools and turns back to liquid water droplets.

Wherever the water finds a way through cracks to the surface, it suddenly and violently boils into steam.

Below ground, hot rocks heat liquid water higher than boiling point, but trap it so it cannot turn to steam.

AMAZING DISCOVERY

Scientist: James Thomson
Discovery: Triple point of water
Date: 1873
The story: Thomson was an engineer specializing in water transport. He showed that pure water can coexist as a solid, liquid, and water vapor at a particular pressure and temperature: 32.01˚F (0.01˚C).

Solid Materials

Most objects are made of solid matter. The atoms or molecules that make up a solid are held together very strongly. There are lots of very different solids, but they all share certain features.

Solid Properties

In some solids, the atoms form regular patterns called crystals. Quartz and salt have a crystal structure. In other solids—for example, polythene—the atoms bond in more of a jumble. Some of these shapeless solids can change shape by stretching—this is called being ductile.

A crystal's shape depends on the arrangement of atoms inside. Its hue depends on the elements involved.

The metal iron is ductile. When it's hot, it can be pulled or hammered into shape.

Inside crystals, atoms can be arranged in cubes, hexagons, pyramids, or diamond shapes.

Crystals such as this quartz form by slowly adding new atoms to the outside edges of a growing structure.

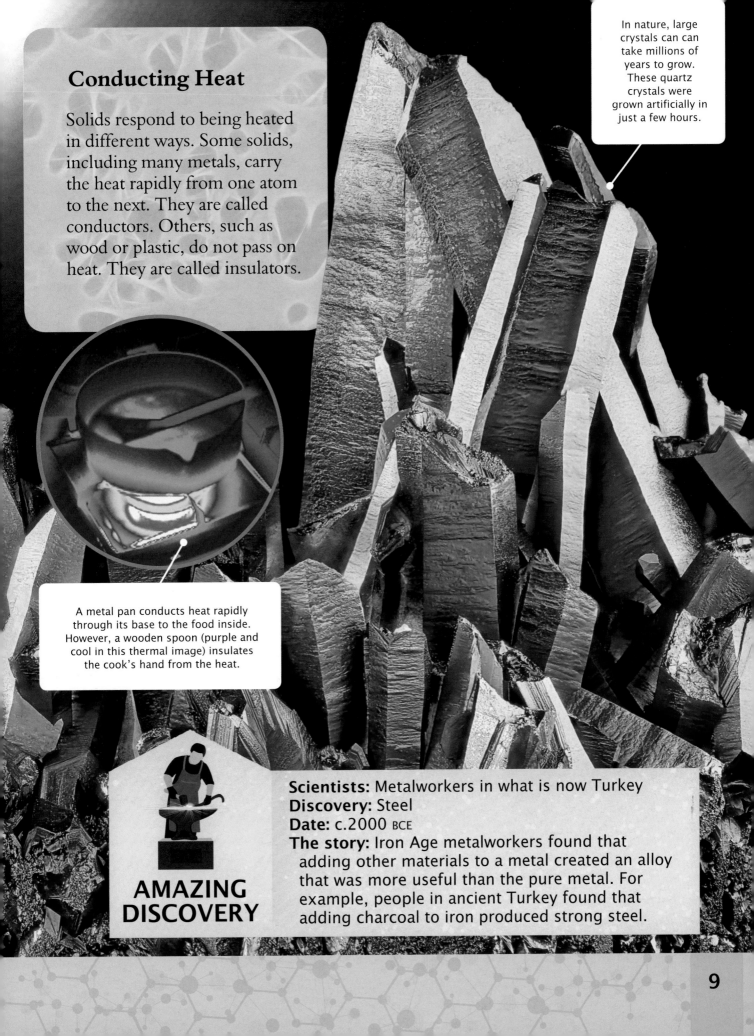

Conducting Heat

Solids respond to being heated in different ways. Some solids, including many metals, carry the heat rapidly from one atom to the next. They are called conductors. Others, such as wood or plastic, do not pass on heat. They are called insulators.

In nature, large crystals can can take millions of years to grow. These quartz crystals were grown artificially in just a few hours.

A metal pan conducts heat rapidly through its base to the food inside. However, a wooden spoon (purple and cool in this thermal image) insulates the cook's hand from the heat.

AMAZING DISCOVERY

Scientists: Metalworkers in what is now Turkey
Discovery: Steel
Date: c.2000 BCE
The story: Iron Age metalworkers found that adding other materials to a metal created an alloy that was more useful than the pure metal. For example, people in ancient Turkey found that adding charcoal to iron produced strong steel.

Liquids and Gases

Most substances are only liquid in a narrow range of temperatures, between their solid and gas phases. Atoms or molecules inside liquids are more loosely bonded than those in solids. In gases, their bonds are even weaker.

Moving Particles

In everyday language, we use "fluid" to mean a liquid. In science, it covers both liquids and gases because their particles can flow more or less freely. Water molecules run very freely but those in molasses are more strongly bonded and flow more slowly. Slow-moving, thick liquids are described as "viscous."

Special photography techniques reveal how the molecules in gases or liquids are constantly moving—for example, in this cough.

Gas Laws

Gases expand to fill the space available. If the gas is contained, its molecules will bounce off the walls of its container, producing pressure. Heating a gas speeds up the movement of its molecules and increases its pressure. Pumping air into a bicycle tire increases the pressure of gas inside, and also raises its temperature.

In cooler weather, the gas molecules in the tire slow down. The pressure reduces and the tire deflates. It has to be pumped up again.

AMAZING DISCOVERY

Scientist: Daniel Bernoulli
Discovery: Bernoulli's principle
Date: 1738
The story: Swiss mathematician Bernoulli discovered that fluids flowing at fast speeds create less pressure than slow-moving ones. The design of an aircraft wing uses this principle to create lift—its shape forces air to move quickly as it passes over its upper surface.

Hot-air balloons work because hot gases rise up through cooler ones. That's because heat moves through fluids by convection—a process where hot parts of the substance expand and flow into colder areas.

The warm air molecules expand and put pressure on the balloon's inner walls so they bulge outward.

The air in the balloon is warmer and lighter than the surrounding cold air, so the balloon floats upward.

Elements

Elements are the most basic substances. They are made up of tiny identical particles called atoms and they cannot be split into simpler substances. Each element's atoms have unique properties.

Properties, Mixtures, and Compounds

There are ninety-four elements found in nature. Seventeen are non-metals. They include carbon, oxygen, and nitrogen. Most of the others are metals, apart from six metalloids—elements that sometimes behave like metals and sometimes like non-metals. Two or more elements can mixed together without their atoms bonding. This is a mixture. They can also be combined in a chemical reaction so that their atoms bond. This is a compound.

An element's melting and boiling points decide whether we find it as a solid, liquid, or gas.

Sulfur combines with other elements to form chemical compounds. When it combines with oxygen from the air it forms sulfur dioxide.

This is a mixture of the elements iron and sulfur. Their atoms have not bonded. The iron atoms are magnetic but the sulfur atoms are not. This makes them easy to separate when a magnet is near.

This is iron sulfide, a compound of iron and sulfur. Its atoms cannot be separated without destroying the compound. Iron sulfide is not magnetic, so none of its atoms are attracted to the magnet.

Pure sulfur can have many different forms, depending on the way its atoms bond to form crystals.

The crater of Ethiopia's Dallol Volcano is covered in sulfur-based chemical compounds, and different forms of pure sulfur.

Atomic Bonds

When atoms bond together, they make larger particles called molecules. The way they bond depends on how many particles called electrons they contain (see page 22). Certain numbers of electrons are more stable than others. Atoms gain or share electrons to reach these stable numbers.

A sodium (Na) atom has one electron in its outer shell. A chlorine (Cl) atom has space for one more. When they bond to form sodium chloride (salt), the sodium gives its outer electron to the chlorine.

When two chlorine (Cl) atoms bond to form a chlorine molecule, they share a pair of electrons. Now each chlorine atom's outer shell has a more stable number of electrons.

AMAZING DISCOVERY

Scientist: John Dalton
Discovery: Atomic theory
Date: 1803
The story: Dalton said that all matter is made of atoms, and that atoms are indivisible and indestructible. He observed that all atoms of a given element have the same properties. He also described how compounds are formed by a combination of two or more different kinds of atom.

Periodic Table

The periodic table is a way to display the properties of all 118 elements that have been discovered so far. It lets chemists predict what characteristics an element has just by knowing where it is in the table.

The shape of the periodic table reflects the arrangement of electrons inside atoms. Electrons are the subatomic particles that control chemical reactions between elements.

Periods and Groups

The elements are arranged in seven rows in order of their atomic number—the number of protons that one atom of that element has in its nucleus. Each row is called a period. Elements that share similar properties are arranged in columns called groups. There are 18 groups.

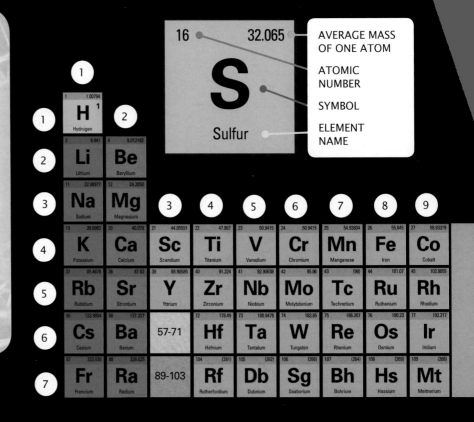

AVERAGE MASS OF ONE ATOM

ATOMIC NUMBER

SYMBOL

ELEMENT NAME

There are too many elements to fit in Period 6 of Group 3, so they are here:

There are too many elements to fit in Period 7 of Group 3, so they are here:

Atoms tend to get heavier from left to right in each period (row), and from top to bottom in each group (column).

KEY
- ALKALI METALS
- ALKALI EARTH METALS
- TRANSITION METALS
- BASIC METALS
- SEMI-METALS
- NON-METALS
- HALOGENS
- NOBLE GASES
- LANTHANIDES
- ACTINIDES

AMAZING DISCOVERY

Scientist: Dmitri Mendeleev
Discovery: The periodic table
Date: 1869
The story: Mendeleev was one of the first chemists to spot repeating patterns in the chemistry of elements with different masses. This let him to draw up the first periodic table and predict the discovery and properties of new elements.

All the elements in a group have the same number of electrons in their outer shell.

New Elements

Scientists can make new elements in special nuclear reactors. They fire extra particles at the central nuclei of the heaviest elements. More than 20 new elements have been made this way, but they are all unstable and fall apart after just a short time. This is why they are not found in nature.

18
2 18.998403 **He** Helium

13	14	15	16	17
5 10.811 **B** Boron	6 12.0107 **C** Carbon	7 14.007 **N** Nitrogen	8 15.9994 **O** Oxygen	9 18.998403 **F** Fluorine	10 20.180 **Ne** Neon

| 10 | 11 | 12 | 13 26.98153 **Al** Aluminum | 14 28.0855 **Si** Silicon | 15 30.974 **P** Phosphorus | 16 32.065 **S** Sulfur | 17 35.453 **Cl** Chlorine | 18 39.948 **Ar** Argon |

| 28 58.6934 **Ni** Nickel | 29 63.546 **Cu** Copper | 30 65.38 **Zn** Zinc | 31 69.723 **Ga** Gallium | 32 72.64 **Ge** Germanium | 33 74.922 **As** Arsenic | 34 78.96 **Se** Selenium | 35 79.904 **Br** Bromine | 36 84.80 **Kr** Krypton |

| 46 106.42 **Pd** Palladium | 47 107.8682 **Ag** Silver | 48 112.441 **Cd** Cadmium | 49 114.818 **In** Indium | 50 118.710 **Sn** Tin | 51 121.760 **Sb** Antimony | 52 127.60 **Te** Tellurium | 53 126.9044 **I** Iodine | 54 131.92 **Xe** Xenon |

| 78 195.084 **Pt** Platinum | 79 195.084 **Au** Gold | 80 200.59 **Hg** Mercury | 81 204.3833 **Tl** Thallium | 82 207.2 **Pb** Lead | 83 208.980 **Bi** Bismuth | 84 (210) **Po** Polonium | 85 (210) **At** Astatine | 86 (220) **Rn** Radon |

| 110 (271) **Ds** Darmstadtium | 111 (272) **Rg** Roentgenium | 112 (285) **Cn** Copernicium | 113 (284) **Nh** Nihonium | 114 (289) **Fl** Flerovium | 115 (288) **Mc** Moscovium | 116 (292) **Lv** Livermorium | 117 (294) **Ts** Tennessine | 118 (294) **Og** Oganesson |

| 63 151.965 **Eu** Europium | 64 157.25 **Gd** Gadolinium | 65 158.92534 **Tb** Terbium | 66 162.50 **Dy** Dysprosium | 67 164.9303 **Ho** Holmium | 68 167.26 **Er** Erbium | 69 168.93421 **Tm** Thulium | 70 173.04 **Yb** Ytterbium | 71 174.967 **Lu** Lutetium |

| 95 (243) **Am** Americium | 96 (247) **Cm** Curium | 97 (247) **Bk** Berkelium | 98 (251) **Cf** Californium | 99 (252) **Es** Einsteinium | 100 (257) **Fm** Fermium | 101 (258) **Md** Mendelevium | 102 (259) **No** Nobelium | 103 (260) **Lr** Lawrencium |

The elements in Group 18 are called the noble gases and are non-reactive. They all have a full outer shell of electrons.

Physicists buil[d] new elements [by] nuclear fusion— the same proce[ss] that combines elements insid[e] the Sun.

1

Rocks and Minerals

Most of Earth's elements are naturally locked up in complex chemical molecules. These form solid substances called minerals, which can have beautiful crystal structures. Most rocks are made up from a mix of different minerals. Some elements, such as gold, prefer not to bond with others, so they can be found naturally in pure form.

Elements in the Earth

The rocks that make up Earth's thin outer crust mostly contain just a few fairly light elements. Heavy elements, including precious metals, tend to sink down toward Earth's core. The main elements in the rocky crust are oxygen (47 percent), silicon (28 percent), aluminum (8 percent), iron (5 percent), and calcium (3.5 percent).

Mineral molecules bond together to form crystals. This agate (a form of silicon dioxide) includes crystals on a range of different scales, some too small to see.

Most useful elements are found as chemical compounds in mineral form. Once they have been mined, we use chemical processes to extract the elements.

Gold does not form minerals. These miners are extracting it in its pure form from "veins" in the rock.

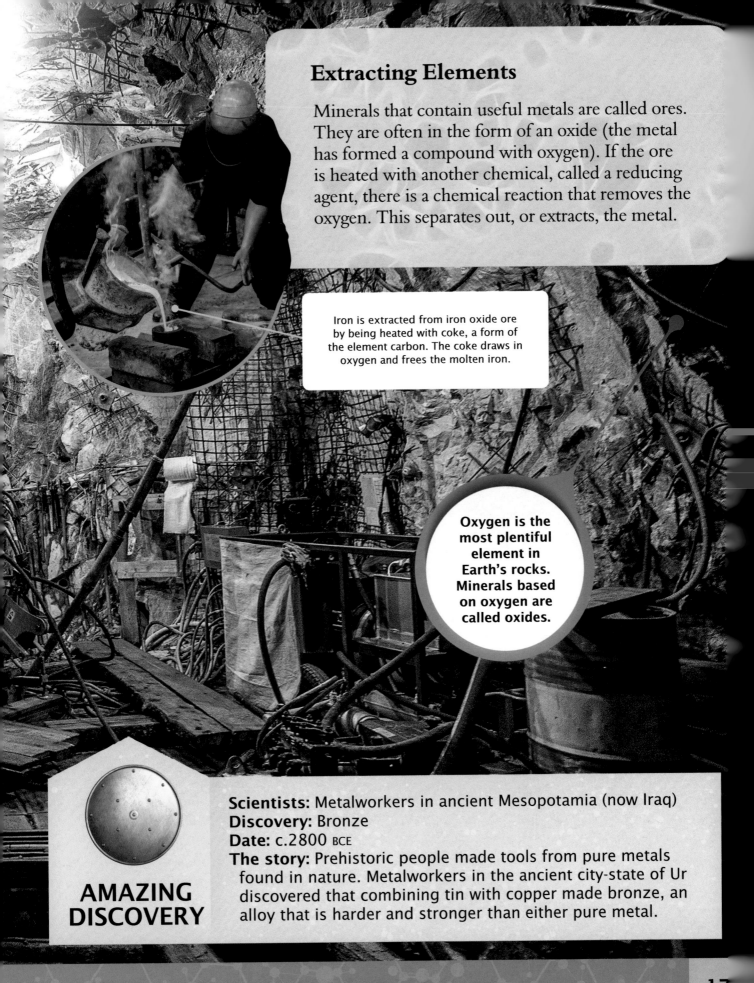

Extracting Elements

Minerals that contain useful metals are called ores. They are often in the form of an oxide (the metal has formed a compound with oxygen). If the ore is heated with another chemical, called a reducing agent, there is a chemical reaction that removes the oxygen. This separates out, or extracts, the metal.

Iron is extracted from iron oxide ore by being heated with coke, a form of the element carbon. The coke draws in oxygen and frees the molten iron.

Oxygen is the most plentiful element in Earth's rocks. Minerals based on oxygen are called oxides.

AMAZING DISCOVERY

Scientists: Metalworkers in ancient Mesopotamia (now Iraq)
Discovery: Bronze
Date: c.2800 BCE
The story: Prehistoric people made tools from pure metals found in nature. Metalworkers in the ancient city-state of Ur discovered that combining tin with copper made bronze, an alloy that is harder and stronger than either pure metal.

Chemistry at Work

Chemical reactions rearrange atoms and molecules to create new substances. The substances at the start of a chemical reaction are called reactants. During the reaction their particles break apart, join together, or swap places. They create a new set of substances called products.

How Reactions Work

All chemical reactions take in or give out energy, often in the form of heat, light, or sound. Combustion is an explosive reaction that produces more energy than it takes in. A catalyst is a substance that speeds up a reaction without using energy, and without changing itself.

Combustion is used for fireworks. Gunpowder reacts with oxygen in the air and releases intense heat and bright light. Adding metal salts gives different effects—strontium carbonate produces red fireworks, barium chloride makes green, and calcium chloride creates orange.

Organic Chemistry

The structure of carbon atoms lets them form four strong chemical bonds—the most of any common element. As a result, carbon combines with itself and other atoms to make many different and complex molecules known as organic chemicals. These include the building blocks of life itself.

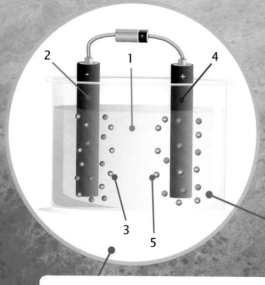

1. Chemicals break apart into positively and negatively charged particles called ions.

2. Negative electrode is a source of electrons.

3. Positive ions combine with electrons to form atoms.

4. Positive electrode draws in electrons.

5. Negative ions give up electrons to form atoms.

Electrolysis uses electrical energy to start a reaction. Electric current is passed through a solution that contains dissolved particles of the reactants.

Seawater is a chemical solution—a mixture of pure water with floating molecules of different chemical compounds.

Chemical reactions are helping to create artificial reefs. The "biorock" forms when a reaction attracts the rocky mineral calcium carbonate to objects—in this case, bikes.

The biorock process is started by electrolysis—passing a small electric current through the seawater.

Corals begin to grow on the build-up of calcium carbonate. Soon, other reef creatures will come.

Scientists: Mikhail Lomonosov, Antoine Lavoisier (left)
Discovery: Balance in reactions
Date: 1748–1774
The story: Chemists Lomonosov and Lavoisier showed that the total mass of substances present before and after a chemical reaction (including any gases released) is the same. This convinced later chemists that reactions involve rearranging fixed numbers of atoms.

AMAZING DISCOVERY

Electrical Properties

Electricity is a form of energy. Every atom has a balance of electric charge in its particles—positive charge in its protons and negative in its electrons. If an atom gains or loses electrons, those charges are no longer balanced. The object becomes electrically charged.

Conductors, Currents, and Circuits

Any electrically charged object has an electromagnetic field around it, which attracts or repels other charged objects. Electricity flows when electrons or other charged particles move. Materials that let electricity flow through them are called electrical conductors. Most metals are good conductors. Charge flowing through a conductor is called an electric current. An electric circuit is a loop of conducting wire that carries current through components with different functions.

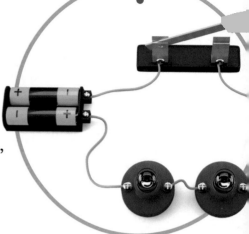

When a switch is closed to complete this circuit, electricity will flow. The current will heat the wire in the lamp so it glows.

A maglev train hovers above the rails, lifted by the repelling force between superconductors and magnets.

The maglev's track is made of very powerful electrical conductors called superconductors.

Maglev is short for "magnetic levitation."

Scientist: Hans-Christian Ørsted
Discovery: Electromagnetic fields
Date: 1820
The story: Danish physicist Ørsted discovered that switching an electric current off and on caused the needle of a nearby magnetic compass to flicker. This was the first evidence that changing currents produce changing magnetic fields around themselves.

Electricity Supply

Electricity from power stations travels along a network of cables. The current travels at high voltages to stop too much power being lost along the way. Devices called transformers step up the voltage as the electricity leaves the power station, and then reduce it to a safe level before it enters our homes, schools, and factories.

Transformers at this electrical substation change high-voltage electricity to suitable lower voltages. Homes need low-voltage electricity, while railways need high voltage.

Coils of conducting wire in the track create an electromagnetic field that pushes the train forward.

Maglev trains like this one in Shanghai can reach speeds of up to 267 mph (430 km/h).

Inside the Atom

Atoms are the building blocks of everyday matter, and the smallest amount of an individual element that can exist. But each atom is made up of even smaller particles. Together, these subatomic particles—protons, neutrons, and electrons—create the atom's overall structure.

Particle Properties

Subatomic particles have particular features. Protons have almost as much mass as a hydrogen atom, and carry a positive electric charge. Neutrons have a similar mass but no electric charge. Electrons have much less mass than the other particles, and carry a negative electric charge equal and opposite to the proton's charge.

This amazing photograph shows tracks left behind by subatomic particles as they move through fluid. Scientists smash atoms together to create subatomic particles.

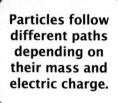

Particles follow different paths depending on their mass and electric charge.

The positive charge of protons (red) in an atom's nucleus is usually balanced by the negative charge of electrons (blue) orbiting around it. Most of the atom's mass comes from a combination of protons and neutrons (white).

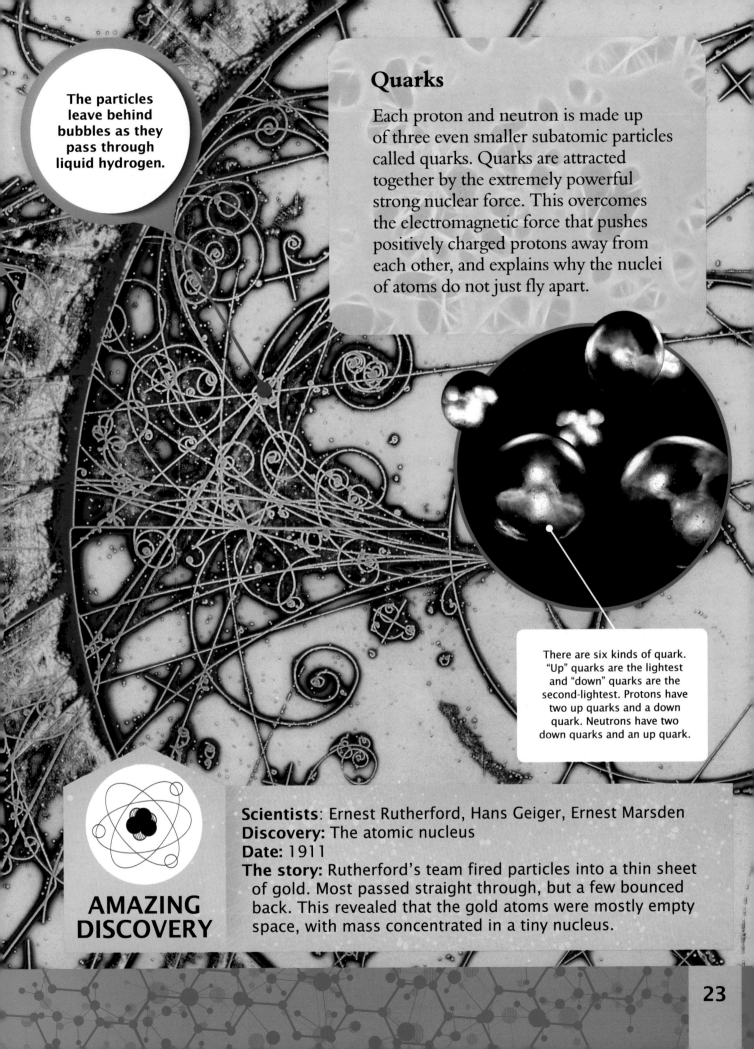

The particles leave behind bubbles as they pass through liquid hydrogen.

Quarks

Each proton and neutron is made up of three even smaller subatomic particles called quarks. Quarks are attracted together by the extremely powerful strong nuclear force. This overcomes the electromagnetic force that pushes positively charged protons away from each other, and explains why the nuclei of atoms do not just fly apart.

There are six kinds of quark. "Up" quarks are the lightest and "down" quarks are the second-lightest. Protons have two up quarks and a down quark. Neutrons have two down quarks and an up quark.

AMAZING DISCOVERY

Scientists: Ernest Rutherford, Hans Geiger, Ernest Marsden
Discovery: The atomic nucleus
Date: 1911
The story: Rutherford's team fired particles into a thin sheet of gold. Most passed straight through, but a few bounced back. This revealed that the gold atoms were mostly empty space, with mass concentrated in a tiny nucleus.

Quantum World

Matter on everyday scales tends to behave in easily predictable ways. We need a very different set of rules, called quantum physics, to describe matter on the very smallest scales and help us guess how atoms and subatomic particles will behave.

Waves or Particles?

The key to quantum physics is a strange idea called wave-particle duality. Very small particles sometimes behave like waves, and we can't measure all their properties accurately at the same time. So if we measure a particle's speed we can't pin down its position, and if we pin down its position we lose track of its speed.

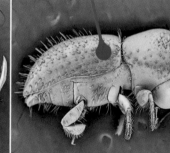

Quantum physics lies behind the electron microscope, which lets us view tiny creatures in huge detail.

Electron microscope images of bugs, ticks, fleas, and other small creatures can magnify details by up to two million times.

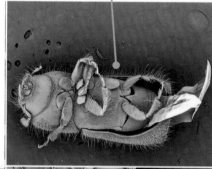

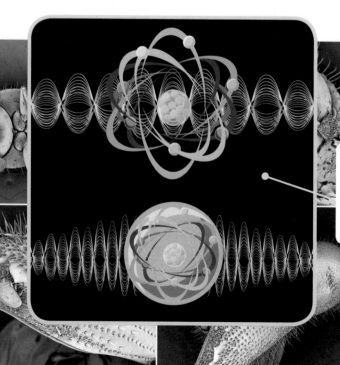

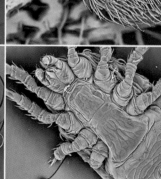

An atom can be viewed as a particle or a wave. The smallest particles (top) have relatively long wavelengths. Larger ones (bottom) have much shorter wavelengths.

AMAZING DISCOVERY

Scientists: Louis de Broglie, Erwin Schrödinger (left)
Discovery: Wave-particle duality
Date: 1924–1926
The story: In 1924, de Broglie suggested that just as light waves can also act like particles, perhaps small particles could behave like waves. Two years later, Schrödinger worked out an equation for describing these waves.

Quantum Physics and the Everyday World

There are lots of uncertainties in quantum physics, but it also answers questions ranging from how stars shine to how plants make energy from sunlight. Many technologies rely on our understanding that subatomic particles can also behave as waves, including nuclear power, solar panels, modern electronics, and lasers.

Electrons have much shorter wavelengths than light waves, so they can pick out finer detail.

Lasers are intense beams of light. They are produced by pumping atoms full of electrical energy so that they produce rapid bursts of photons (light waves).

Fun Facts

Now that you have discovered lots about matter and materials, boost your knowledge further with these 10 quick facts!

The metal mercury is usually in liquid form. Its freezing point is –37.8°F (–38.8°C) and its boiling point is 674°F (356.7°C), both the lowest of any metal.

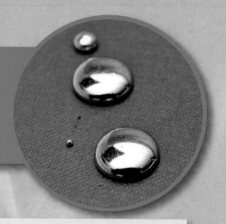

Tungsten, used in high-performance aircraft, has the highest melting point of any metal. It remains solid up to an amazing 6,277°F (3,414°C).

Solid carbon dioxide, or "dry ice," can change straight from being a solid to a gas without passing through a liquid phase at all.

Oxygen is Earth's most common element. Most is locked up in rocks—it accounts for 47 percent of the mass of Earth's crust.

Atoms of oganesson, the heaviest element, are so unstable that they disintegrate in less than one-thousandth of a second.

Nearly all the rocks and minerals on Earth started out in liquid lava erupted from volcanoes. The only exceptions are meteorites—rocks that fell from space.

Baking a muffin involves chemical reactions. Heat helps the baking powder create bubbles of gas so the muffin rises, and it changes the protein in the egg so the muffin's firm.

Electricity from batteries is direct current (DC)—it flows in one direction. Electrical sockets provide alternating current (AC) that changes direction many times a second.

If an atom of hydrogen (the simplest element) was blown up to the size of a soccer stadium, its central nucleus would be no larger than a pea!

An electron wave has a wavelength 300–500 times smaller than a light wave.

Your Questions Answered

We know an incredible amount about the building blocks that form our world and life itself. But there is always more to discover. Scientists are still researching elements, atoms, molecules, and their building blocks, and are continuing to find out more incredible details. Here are some questions about materials and matter that can help you understand more about this vast and fascinating topic.

What is a particle accelerator?

Physicists often use particle accelerators to examine the properties of atomic and subatomic particles. Cern, in Switzerland, has the largest accelerator, called the Large Hadron Collider, which is a ring-shaped set of tubes, underground. Scientists send particles around these tubes at incredibly high speeds and make them collide to study their make-up and how they behave under extreme conditions. They have also discovered a number of particles, including the Higgs boson.

Why is subatomic particle research important?

The science of subatomic particles is complex, and can appear very abstract. But although it may seem that way, subatomic particles are key to our understanding of how the world works, and how life itself developed on our planet. Knowing as much as possible about the smallest building blocks of our planet helps us understand the bigger picture, too.

Every new insight into subatomic particles and how they behave offers a new understanding of the world around us.

Have all elements been discovered?

The short answer to this question is "no." It is likely that the elements that are stable and occur naturally have all been discovered by now. However, there are a number of elements that scientists initially thought they were "creating" in their laboratories and that didn't exist in nature. These are highly instable elements that form and then disintegrate in a very short space of time. Further research has revealed that even elements such as these can occur naturally—often in radioactive materials. So there may be many more to discover.

Which minerals are found in meteorites?

Every day, tiny rocks from space find their way to our planet. If they manage to land on the planet's surface, we call them meteorites. Scientists estimate that about 48.5 tons (44,000 kg) of meteoritic material falls to Earth every single day! This introduces a lot of extra-terrestrial material, some of which is in mineral form. Scientists have discovered that some minerals are more common in meteorites that they are in Earth's crust. These include whitlockite, chromite, and certain kinds of serpentine.

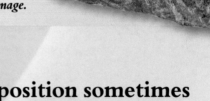

Meteorites are mostly fist-sized or smaller, and even though so many land on the Earth's surface, they hardly ever cause damage.

Does deposition sometimes occur naturally?

The process of a material changing its phase from gas to solid without initial condensation is called deposition. There are few examples of this happening in nature, but one common example is when water vapor meets a freezing cold windowpane and immediately turns to ice.

The ice crystals that form through deposition often freeze in pretty patterns.

Glossary

atom The smallest possible particle of a chemical element.

compound A substance formed from two or more elements that are chemically bound together.

conductor The solid object through which heat moves from its hotter part to its colder one.

convection The movement of heat through a liquid or gas caused by hot material rising.

crystal A solid where the molecules are organised in a repeating pattern.

ductile When a solid can be stretched and manipulated to change shape.

electron A negatively charged particle found in all atoms.

element A substance that cannot be broken down into simpler substances.

fluid In science, a substance that has no fixed shape, such as a liquid or gas.

insulator A substance that does not easily conduct either heat or sound.

mineral A solid, natural, inorganic substance.

molecule A group of atoms bonded together to form what is known as a chemical compound. A molecule is the smallest particle that still has all of the chemical properties of a substance.

neutron A particle that is subatomic (smaller than an atom) and has no electric charge.

nucleus The positively charged core of an atom.

proton The positively charged particle that can be found in an atomic nucleus.

quark A subatomic particle carrying an electric charge.

viscous Having a thick, sticky quality, somewhere between liquid and solid.

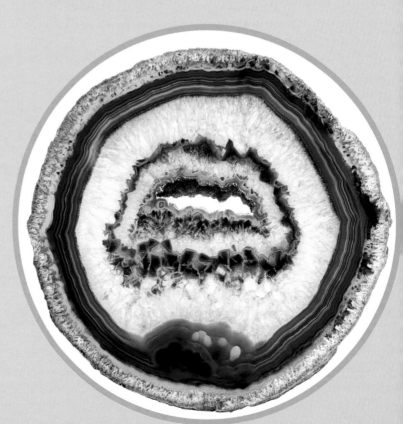

Further Information

BOOKS

Arbuthnott, Gill. *A Beginner's Guide to the Periodic Table.* London, UK:
  A & C Black, 2014.

Guinness World Records. *Science & Stuff.* London, UK: Guinness World Records
  Limited, 2018

Ignotofsky, Rachel. *Women In Science: 50 Fearless Pioneers Who Changed The World.*
  London, UK: Wren and Rook, 2017.

Mould, Steve. *How To Be A Scientist.* London, UK: DK Children, 2017.

Richards, Jon and Ed Simkins. *Science In Infographics: Materials.* London, UK:
  Wayland Books, 2017.

WEBSITES

Changing Materials
https://www.bbc.com/education/topics/zcvv4wx
Explore this BBC webpage and find out much more about materials and their states.

DCPS Rocks and Minerals Cornerstone
https://learninglab.si.edu/collections/dcps-rocks-and-minerals-cornerstone
/s1ELacmBNcegUVko#r
Head to the Smithsonian Learning Lab and learn all about different minerals.

Materials Around Us
http://www.thunderboltkids.co.za/Grade4/02-matter-and-materials/chapter1.html
Explore activities that investigate material properties.

Index

A
atom 4, 5, 6, 8, 9, 10, 12, 13, 14, 18, 19, 20, 22, 23, 24, 25, 26, 27, 28

B
Bernoulli, Daniel 11
boil 6, 7, 12, 26

C
carbon dioxide 26
compound 12, 13, 16, 17, 19
condensation 6, 29
conductor 9, 20
convection 11
crystal 8, 9, 12, 16, 29

D
Dalton, John 13
de Broglie, Louis 25
deposition 6, 29
ductile 8

E
electricity 4, 20, 21, 27
electromagnetic 20, 21, 23
electron 5, 13, 14, 15, 18, 19, 22, 24, 25, 27
element 8, 12–13, 14, 15, 16, 17, 18, 22, 26, 27, 28, 29
energy 4, 6, 18, 20, 25
evaporation 6

F
fluid 10, 11, 22
freezing 6, 26, 29

G
gas 4, 6, 10–11, 12, 14, 15, 19, 25, 26, 27, 29
Geiger, Hans 23

I
insulator 9

L
Lavoisier, Antoine 19
liquid 4, 6, 7, 10–11, 12, 23, 26, 27
Lomonosov, Mikhail 19

M
maglev train 20, 21
magnetic 12, 20, 21
Marsden, Ernest 23
melting 6, 12, 26
Mendeleev, Dmitri 15
metal 8, 9, 12, 14, 15, 16, 17, 18, 20, 26
mineral 16–17, 19, 27, 29
molecule 6, 8, 10, 11, 13, 16, 18, 19, 28

N
neutron 22, 23
nucleus 14, 22, 23, 27

O
ore 17
Ørsted, Hans-Christian 21
oxygen 12, 15, 16, 17, 18, 26

P
particle 5, 6, 10, 12, 13, 14, 15, 18, 20, 22, 23, 24, 25, 28
phase 6–7, 10, 26, 29
pressure 7, 10, 11
proton 14, 20, 22, 23

Q
quantum physics 24–25
quark 23

R
reaction (chemical) 4, 12, 14, 17, 18, 19, 27
Rutherford, Ernest 23

S
Schrödinger, Erwin 25
solid 4, 6, 7, 8, 9, 10, 12, 16, 26, 29
subatomic 5, 14, 22, 23, 24, 25, 28
sublimation 6

T
Thomson, James 7

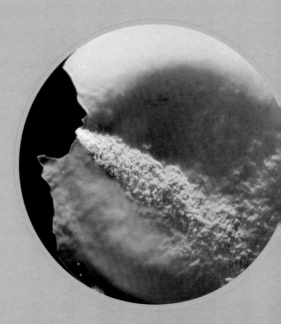